Community Places

Library

by Amy McDonald

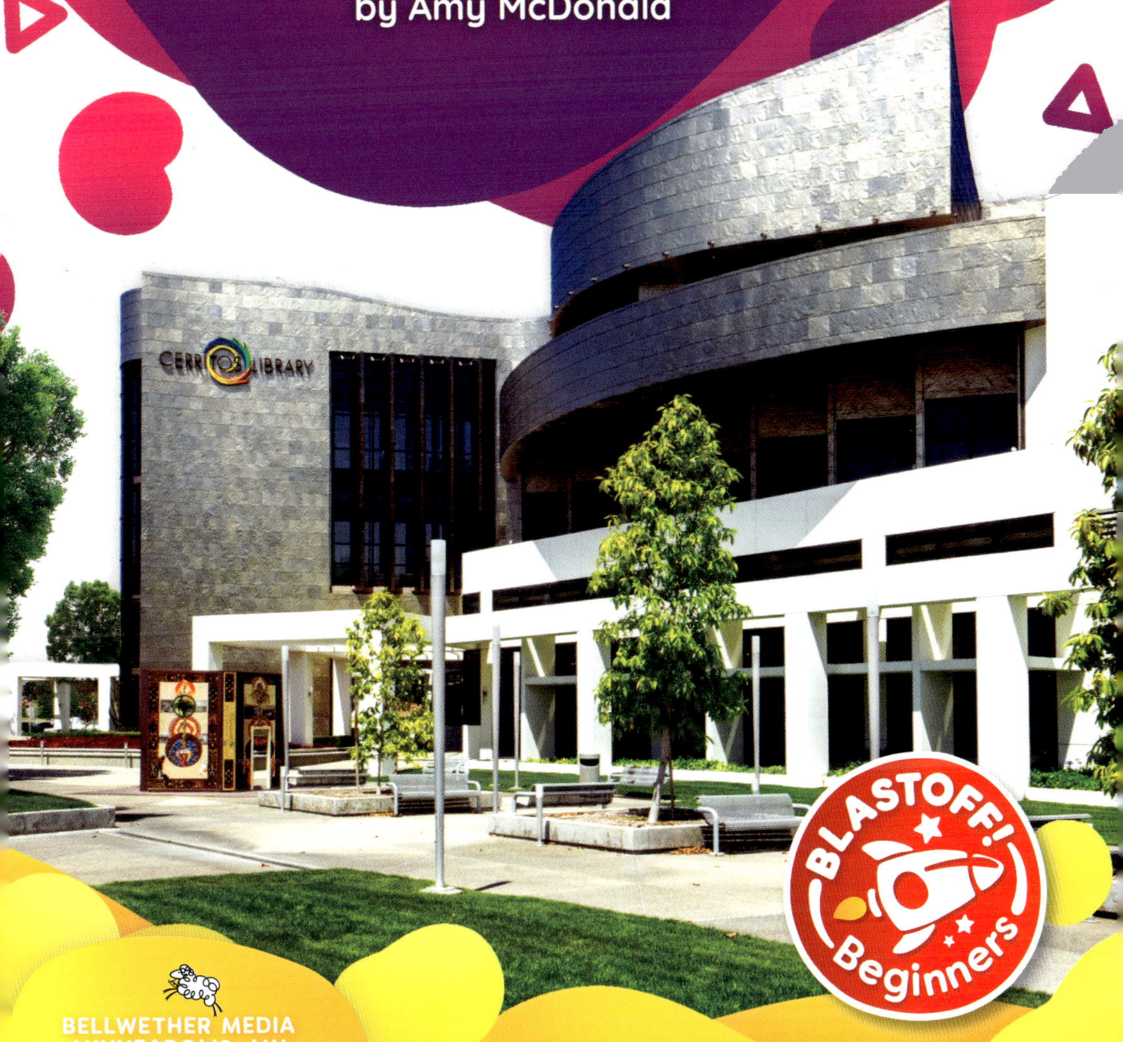

Blastoff! Beginners

BELLWETHER MEDIA
MINNEAPOLIS, MN

Blastoff! Beginners are developed by literacy experts and educators to meet the needs of early readers. These engaging informational texts support young children as they begin reading about their world. Through simple language and high frequency words paired with crisp, colorful photos, Blastoff! Beginners launch young readers into the universe of independent reading.

Sight Words in This Book

a	for	I	so	to
and	get	is	the	use
are	go	look	there	where
at	has	out	they	
can	have	people	this	
do	help	play	time	

This edition first published in 2022 by Bellwether Media, Inc.

Library of Congress Cataloging-in-Publication Data

Names: McDonald, Amy, 1985- author.
Title: Library / by Amy McDonald.
Description: Minneapolis, MN : Bellwether Media, Inc., 2022. | Series: Blastoff! Beginners. Community places | Includes bibliographical references and index. | Audience: Ages PreK-2. | Audience: Grades K-1.
Identifiers: LCCN 2021044252 (print) | LCCN 2021044253 (ebook) | ISBN 9781644875674 (library binding) | ISBN 9781648346583 (paperback) | ISBN 9781648345784 (ebook)
Subjects: LCSH: Libraries--Juvenile literature. | Librarians--Juvenile literature.
Classification: LCC Z665.5 .M367 2022 (print) | LCC Z665.5 (ebook) | DDC 027--dc23
LC record available at https://lccn.loc.gov/2021044252
LC ebook record available at https://lccn.loc.gov/2021044253

Editor: Christina Leaf Designer: Andrea Schneider

Printed in the United States of America, North Mankato, MN.

Table of Contents

At the Library!

Where can I get books to read? The library!

What Are Libraries?

Libraries are quiet places. People go to **browse** books.

books

browsing

There is a lot to do at the library. Anyone can go!

Learning at the Library

Libraries have tables. People work and study.

table

They have computers. People read and play games.

computer

They have **shelves**. People look for books.

shelves

They have a desk. People ask **librarians** for help.

librarian
desk

People check out books to take home. They use library cards.

library
card

This library
has story time.
Libraries have
so much to offer!

Library Facts

Inside a Library

What Happens in a Library?

read

play computer games

check out books

Glossary

browse

to look through

librarians

the people in charge at the library

shelves

flat places above the floor that hold books

To Learn More

ON THE WEB

FACTSURFER

Factsurfer.com gives you a safe, fun way to find more information.

1. Go to www.factsurfer.com.
2. Enter "library" into the search box and click 🔍.
3. Select your book cover to see a list of related content.

Index

The images in this book are reproduced through the courtesy of: Debbie Eckert, front cover; Africa Studio, p. 3; Anna Om, p. 4; all_about_people, pp. 4-5; Vladimir Nikitin, p. 6; wavebreakmedia, pp. 6-7, 14-15; Jason Ligon, pp. 8-9; Jacek Chabraszewski, p. 10; LightFieldStudios, pp. 10-11; Rozhnovskaya Tanya, p. 12; Ermolaev Alexander, pp. 12-13; Johnathan21, p. 14; Tyler Olson, pp. 16-17, 23 (librarians); SDI Productions, pp. 18-19, 22 (inside, check out books); monkeybusinessimages, pp. 20-21; anek.soowannaphoom, p. 22 (read); ESB Professional, p. 22 (play computer games); JGA, p. 23 (browse); Cheryle Myers, p. 23 (shelves).